SIFTING THROUGH PIECES

Lachlan Kempson

BookLeaf Publishing

India | USA | UK

Presentation by BookLeaf Publishing

Web: www.bookleafpub.com

E-mail: info@bookleafpub.com

ISBN: 9789358360509

First edition 2021

To my family, for your support, your love, and the inspiration
you give to me just by being who you are.

And to Ashlea, for believing in every piece of writing I have
ever done, and for encouraging me to believe in it too. Thank
you for who you are, and who you help me to be.

HORIZON

I can see no farther

than that mark in the distance.

I know its nature,

not what lies beyond;

is it a blemish?

The tide laps at the shore,

cyclical,

my ankles in the sand,

but my heart out at sea.

The waves abound

and obey only their rhythm;

chaos and calm.

Those who've searched before

claim the distant mark is no more at an end

than I am,

but that is the fright.

Desolate:

that's how it looks from here.

I wonder if that's how I look from there.

Can I be seen on the other side?

Assuming such a thing

exists.

No explorer has ever returned

from beyond;

bodies have, of course,

with same handshakes and hugs

and smiles at lovers,

but every wayward soul is lost;

water agitates the human chrysalis

and born is something new:

magic I cannot possess

while anchored on this side.

Maybe the tide will cease to rise,

and I will slip these seaside chains

to burst forth unto that distance.

EDITED

When I write, I try to keep it ordered,

measure the words that are put to page,

shrouding myself in a calmness I don't own.

Words reaching eyes are crafted with a deft hand;

I am no more poet than potter,

fashioning syntactical closeness and wiping away

what strays from the grand design.

You read a produced grace,

but I am attacked by the shadows of words

I mauled: the ones that didn't measure up,

ill-fitting not in nature, but only in my grasp.

Writer and ravager.

I desire the river of language, where expression

drifts leisurely and unstrained,

but my hands intercede:

a manufactured salvation of my splintered

sentences,

(unnecessarily provided, received without thought)

reducing that which binds us

to brokenness.

EVERYONE HAS A JAR

a grimy lid holds closed the jar / plentiful dust / rusted steel / with the faintest of fingertips left behind / the lid is tightly wound down / but the glass is thin / one false move could spill the contents / my entombed imagination / cast out onto the highest shelf / covered by my books and shrouded in the greater imaginary of other minds / inferior / it must stay carefully repressed / a crack in the confines would infect / pages upon pages / prose and poetics / what havoc the release of the untamed wild would cause /

but what release could it proffer my soul?

REVOLUTION

Why is hair so often auburn?

Or the air cool and crisp,

light streaming through windows,

and the grass eternally covered

in its layer of morning dew?

All of it repeated, abused; overruling

the special that they are meant to encapsulate.

And there is meaning:

the search and the asphyxiation

of being unable to define it.

Are we at all immune to this curse:

this elegiac recycling of our concerns? Where is the

freshness –

caught up in the jumble

of phrases that can't be puzzled together;

an unfinished thousand-piece,

their edges too jagged and rough,

and too many pieces missing.

They say, when the inevitable block hits

to return to the roots of your breathing;

find footing in the fundamentals

before trekking for the summit. But

the noise is great, and ceaseless,

hindering our senses and breaking

the bridge between word and being;

what I feel kept unknown -

forced to sit in the cerebral anteroom,

before higher order calls me in. I am master

of none, neither heart nor mind,

bending to their unspoken calls

like a branch in a hurricane,

but even the wind still demands

to be heard. There is beauty in that

and in everything, but in what is there beauty

that no one has yet found?

I cannot paint the sunset over sea

as undiscovered,

nor do I live for rediscovery of things,

moments that pass and coalesce

to reform in my head, special intrinsically,

but not in a way that has never been said.

My heartbreak is laid plain:

how to make the old new again.

RUSTIC PASSAGE

There is a road that I dream of often,

one that I found so many years back

that I wonder if it might still be there;

where trees skirted the bitumen surface

(the sound of the cars did soften),

and holding Autumnal leaves its purpose.

Back then, I was too young to drive

which is honestly probably a good thing,

because in those trees was a magic that held

my focus – a distinctive natural grandeur

(manifesting the colours of the world alive) –

and I wanted nothing to distract from my awe.

I hope that one day I can walk,

or drive, or run, or dance, through again

that last good stretch of quiet.

I know that there is peace there

(though I've forgotten how to get back),

down that comforting thoroughfare.

Unusual for a soul so young to notice only the road,

but it was driven at the exact right time:

when leaves were cascading and the world in bloom,

an isolated tint collection, punctuating the grey

(that I notice more now that I'm grown)

and reminding that it all returns despite decay.

It connected some unknown place in my history

to another where I was going,

but the journey may have been circuitous,

only leading me back to where I began

(to starve out my feeling desultory),

to find that enchanted road again.

IN THE GARDEN

the trees tower overhead;

magpies chatter by our heels

in their trademark song of famine.

In half-shade, the verdant lawns

expose themselves with mottled browns

and harsh rubble.

There is one stone that has settled

peacefully under my elbow,

with a rug the only solace

preventing its piercing edge

from seeing through its purpose.

Small petals, expelled from previous homes,

give their presence to the greenery,

dyeing the world in variety;

their scent a little muted, I wish

for a smidge more sensation,

or that I could be seated atop these

wooden pillars, and touch ether.

But all of these myriad pieces

may as well have been missing,

because of the one:

elegantly poised on the rug,

giggling at the magpie warble,

luminous beneath the tree line gaze —

the one who colours the scene

and renders the arid alive;

the only matter that matters

in the garden.

THE LEXICAL APATHETIC

What if one day the words all go? What if

we wake up, and they've vanished;

realised our indifference and said

'stuff them,'

deciding they miss the old times,

when they were revered and whole –

before we took the shears to them, before we

cut out their fullness and cast them

into the furnace to make them more malleable.

What will they do when they have finally

had enough? Can we

make more? But what if

they erase themselves from us

retroactively, like we never had them

at all;

stripping away not surface

but substructure, the bedrock

and basis and —

how could we make more words

without them?

Where could we go,

and honestly, where would we be

without our allies linguistic?

No voices would be dulcet,

or jarring or calming or shrill;

all our tones would be empty, existing

just to exist, with nothing to tell.

Nothing to make us tremble in fear,

or fall with affection, the sounds

of our laughter lost

in the world if we drove away words.

EVENING IN MY BACKYARD

Bathed in gold, saturated

in a way few things are.

Simple day sky, a cloud

or more, obscuring its blue;

a marred canvas,

but building to a joy

of gradated transcendence,

whispered into life.

Breathed into an atmospheric chrysalis,

crescendoing into magnificence.

Setting only to live and set,

to live and set again.

It refuses time wasting,

pulling perceptual theft of our depth

and easy sensation.

Shadows blend the world into sameness.

18

Its ephemeral last is breathed

too soon.

(for now)

SEASONS

We, like the earth's crowning floral cover,

are known to bloom under sun,

at times when it doesn't beat down but nourishes;

when rays don't burn

but recover

our hearts, and dredge them out of ice and snow,

to melt them as does the hand of a lover;

the melting given as a gift to be

a feeling in the skin

and below.

Our lives are lived in a stunning blaze

of energy perfected under the lights

of the sky in good times, though eventually

it comes in reductions

to raze,

and send us barrelling into the caverns

we have built up for the frost, when

outside seems a treacherous menace

and we stick instead

                              to our patterns.

Those wintry blasts come hurtling often

and all the more when we are locked away,

and cannot see the re-emergence of sun,

and its desire to heal

                              and soften.

12AM

I long for the twinkle of the stars,

before the world felt the need

to mirror the magnificence back;

when artificiality was a slur and not

modus operandi; before we were

living so fast and still

stuck in place, forgetting:

(breath)

there is more to this world

than what we have made.

Before we knew instantaneity,

we humbled ourselves beneath those

luminous firmament anchors,

and our time wasn't this erratic mess

of waiting and having,

defined by presence and absence;

22

it was just steady.

I long for this,

a time that I have never seen

and likely never will,

but I feel its faint whispers

in the darkest pockets of twilight.

SEASIDES AND SHORELINES

It all returns to sea;

these waves that cascade and crash

with spirits that are free;

as gulls whistle in sunset glee

to our beachside chips they dash

before they return to sea.

And before her, before me:

this wildlife unlashed

with spirits completely free

to jump from sand to tree,

returning to make a splash

and rippling in returns to sea.

In awe of the sights I'll always be

until it hits me like a flash:

is my spirit (like theirs) free?

But these thoughts are made temporary

when the shore receives the clash

of breakers and swells of spirits free,

that still both return to sea.

HELD

She sings a graceful song,

calling me beyond my body

to dwell in tethered comfort

by the banks of patient flow,

where nature's buzzing is not

monotony

but distilled joy;

and her hand is made of softness,

clasped by a coarse palm

but carried gently in my heart.

CLUTTER

Empty words don't like to leave:

they love to burrow deeper

and nestle in grey matter's cradle,

tickled by the voltaic sprints

of trying to find their replacements.

TEMPORALITY

Our traces are lost in time,

succeeded in cycles of

new and old,

new and old.

But pieces always cling:

in the taste of sweet drinks;

rainy midnight air's essence;

textures of conversation

between these disparate voices.

Moments given life

in perpetual impermanence,

repeating like the cycles —

becoming old, and new again.

THESE FITTED PIECES

When these pieces come together,

affixing by the edges and layering in arms,

I love to watch this artwork unfold,

building a spreading peace.

From my breath and my breathing,

to picturesque healing,

you carry me.

You create in me no vacancies,

suffusing my idle space with restoration,

and I can see the surrounds forming

in new bits each day, moving outwards

and onwards into the next.

I hope I always read these edges right,

these parallel links to build

the picture fully formed;

our puzzle complete.

DREAM THIEF

In half-sleep's early watch,

I am caught trying to remove

pieces of this coming feature

off of the reel;

to smuggle them over

to this side, becoming truth —

bringing the dreamscape life

into material ideal.

The keepers refuse sharing:

'This movie is for eyes closed viewing.'

But I'd rather it be missed that side

to savour the dream with open-eyed feel.

THE ONE WITH THE WHITE FENCE

Brick and timber coalesce to form a periphery

around even more of their brethren

wrought in close relationship,

like the natives who call this one home;

a furry head awaits arrivals,

peaking between gate palings, giving

a soft welcome to all,

but particularly his known;

diverging characters converge within,

the walls hosting celebrations of connection

through beautiful variance —

in image and memory;

around the table, daily episodes

recounted in light laughs, and sometimes necessary

shadow, but with these people

all eventually becomes light again;

so much life we have bound into this space

surrounding movements and moments

that make up our special spot:

this place that we call our home.

GRAND DESIGNS

That swell of passion,

it brings life to dull schematics:

the early skeleton, these bare bones

of verse. Fervour donates its jolt

to blueprints, transforming page

into purpose and rhythm; curing

and calling to the surface our stories

till now inscribed only in vein.

A JULY EVENING

Winter is forgotten in the midst

of shared warmth,

biting cold rendered toothless against

the comfort of our affections.

Everything is that little bit brighter

on nights like this: when giggles and grins

live perpetually,

and joy nestles where hearts connect

to celebrate in harmonic waves.

RESTORE

When you find the course of flow disrupted,

remove your hand from its conscious stream;

watch it reconstitute and rectify. Water

returns to water at intervention's end

and propels eternally ahead.